PowerKiDS
Readers

Fun Fish

RAYS

Maddie Gibbs

PowerKiDS
press™

New York

Published in 2014 by The Rosen Publishing Group, Inc.
29 East 21st Street, New York, NY 10010

First Edition

Editor: Amelie von Zumbusch
Book Design: Andrew Povolny

Photo Credits: Cover Comstock/Comstock Images/Getty Images; p. 5 StudioSmart/Shutterstock.com; p. 7 Predrag Vuckovic/E+/Getty Images; p. 9 Franco Banfi/WaterFrame/Getty Images; p. 11 Rich Carey/Shutterstock.com; p. 13 Reinhard Dirscherl/WaterFrame/Getty Images; p. 15 Jeff Rotman/Peter Arnold/Getty Images; p. 17 Lawrence Naylor/Photo Researchers/Getty Images; p. 19 Michael AW/Lonely Planet Images/Getty Images; p. 21 Iliuta Goean/Shutterstock.com; p. 23 Comstock/Thinkstock.

Library of Congress Cataloging-in-Publication Data

Gibbs, Maddie.
  Rays / by Maddie Gibbs. — First edition.
    pages cm — (Powerkids readers. Fun fish)
  Includes bibliographical references and index.
  ISBN 978-1-4777-0762-3 (library binding) — ISBN 978-1-4777-0857-6 (pbk.) —
ISBN 978-1-4777-0858-3 (6-pack)
  1. Rays (Fishes)—Juvenile literature. I. Title.
  QL638.8.G53 2014
  597.3'5–dc23
                                           2013000205

Manufactured in the United States of America

CPSIA Compliance Information: Batch #S13PK4: For Further Information contact Rosen Publishing, New York, New York at 1-800-237-9932

Contents

Rays are fish.

They are smart.

They can be big.

Some can sting.

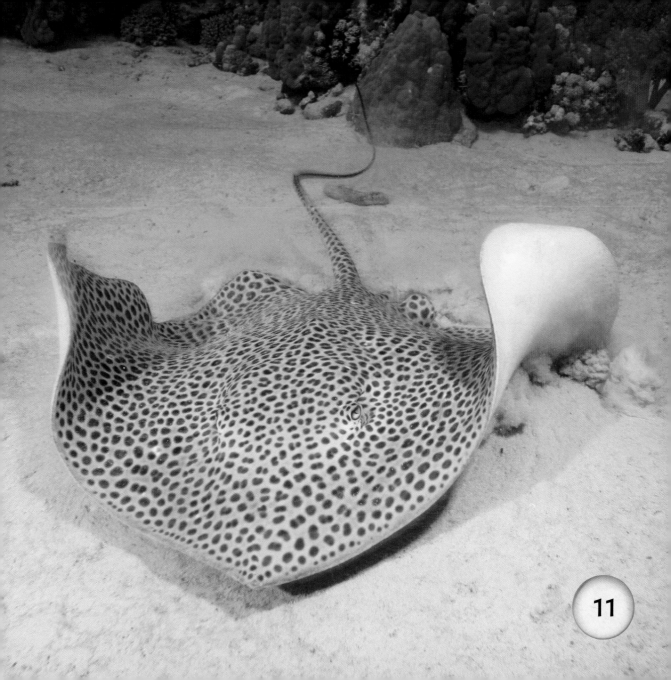

11

A group is a **fever**.

A baby is a **pup**.

Bat rays can live for
24 years.

Manta rays are the biggest kind.

Round rays live in the Pacific Ocean.

Rays are cool!

WORDS TO KNOW

fever

pup

ray

INDEX

WEBSITES

Due to the changing nature of Internet links, PowerKids Press has developed an online list of websites related to the subject of this book. This site is updated regularly. Please use this link to access the list:
www.powerkidslinks.com/pkrff/ray/